It's a Matron of Honor

The Journey to Womanhood

Motivator
Mikkita L Moore

It's a Matron of Honor... Journey to Womanhood

It's a Matron of Honor... Journey to Womanhood

Invisible
DAUGHTER LLC

ISBN: 978-1-7354792-0-0
Imprint: Invisible Daughter, LLC
Printed and bounded in the United States of America.

It's a Matron of Honor... Journey to Womanhood

Thank You!!

It's a Matron of Honor... Journey to Womanhood

Special Thanks & Dedication

Thank all of you for making this book possible

All the Authors: *Mikkita Moore, Latonya Willett, Meighan Cole, Cutrina Oliver, Laina Chelle, and Q.R. Williams-Oakes!!*

Foreword Writer: *Dr. Shaniqua Jones, Thank You so much for accepting the calling of an amazing PERSON and Sister!*

Graphic Designer: *Shawn Robinson, of 727 Marketing... It's been a pleasure to work with you!!*

This book is dedicated to all the ladies that is or has taken that amazing Journey to Womanhood... This one is for you!

Table of Contents

It's a Matron of Honor... Journey to Womanhood

Foreword

When asked to provide the foreword for The Journey to Womanhood, I immediately asked God to give me the right words to set the tone for the journey we are all about to embark together. I know many of us equate womanhood to motherhood but we would be sadly mistaken if we solidified this assumption. We are more than mothers - we are conquerors. The level of resilience and courage it takes to walk a block, not a mile in our shoes are insurmountable as it relates to being - being a woman.

To take a step back, I recently went live on my personal Facebook page and the moment I saw Mikkita's name pop up, I began to speak to her as if she was the only person watching and responding to my live video. As I reflect and recall the moment we had via Facebook, I mentioned how resilient she is; especially during a time where her daily routine was abruptly disrupted due to an extensive injury. God placed it on my heart to speak directly to her spirit in hopes of uplifting and supporting my fellow sister. God needed her to be still and hear His voice. Oftentimes, as women, we are wearing one too many hats and trying to stay afloat. Yes, the incident was unfortunate. No, we definitely do not want to experience pain in order to be still. Yet, God knows His children.

Mikkita, this word is for you. This word is for the many souls that will be touched by you and the other women's transparency. Just like God knows how to reach you, He knows how to reach others. He will use the words in this book to provide narrative healing for others. The resilience and courage I mentioned in the beginning of this foreword is the same resilience and courage taken to help others along The Journey of Womanhood.

As you navigate each word, sentence, page, and chapter, I want us all to delve deep into the ways in which we still seek healing. As His word states in Isaiah 41;10 - Fear not, for I *am* with you; Be not dismayed, for I *am* your God. I will strengthen you. Yes, I will help you. I will uphold you with My righteous right hand. When everything else fails, when COVID-19 attacks the world, when racism; the deadliest virus of the world attempts to continuously enslave us and silence our voices, when our world that was deemed normal is uprooted, please know that God made you a woman - a woman of great courage.

Welcome to The Journey of Womanhood!

Dr. Shaniqua Jones

It's a Matron of Honor... Journey to Womanhood

It's a Matron of Honor... Journey to Womanhood

Chapter One

The Uneasy Journey

Mikkita L. Moore

Mikkita Moore, an author, motivational speaker and mother of five, starting at the tender age of 14 from the South Side of Chicago. Mikkita is a retired, master stylist and cosmetology instructor. She has owned two successful hair salons over a period of 13 years and an event-planning company, *Symply Plyzurez Eventz* since 2004. Mikkita is the CEO of Invisible Daughter LLC, which is the publishing company that specializes in Transparency writing, "Getting the Story Out". Mikkita is also the Founder and CEO of *The Art of Transparency, NFP* an organization with a mission to "Heal ONE Person, One City, ONE State, ONE Nation at a time". Although passionate about teaching others about her journey which includes forgiving a father that wasn't, in her opinion, able to be the model man she had desperately needed as a young girl growing into womanhood, she continued to struggle with her inner feelings. Being able to convey these imbedded emotions is also comforting for her. Learning the *Art of Transparency* is equivalent to facing and being fully aware of who she is, her ability to candidly speak from the heart about real life issues and how to conquer life's trials is one of my greatest gifts.

Speaking to participants is a time for meaningful engagement. Time used to encourage, lead and offer real life situations and results to enable listeners to truly understand and connect with her, not only as the speaker but to have empathy for the topic. One of the results that Mikkita obtains when speaking to audiences is her dynamic ability to ignite an awakening within those who hear her story. It allows them to realize and understand their issue more clearly, that she has been through similar situations and how they, too, can overcome the feelings and possible stagnations from its impact. These processes are all facilitated with audience in mind.

How beneficial it is to have the skill to ignite the path of change. Mikkita's niche is engaging her teen pregnancy and parenting audiences with realistic topics that help identify the issues and the teens' willingness to work towards resolutions. Her books, *The Letter From, the Invisible Daughter* as well as *The Cause and Effect of The Invisible Daughter*, talks about, among other topics, parenting a child that's different from the rest and her doubts of being a good mother. As she speaks candidly about her thoughts of suicide and being in unsafe relationships that included domestic violence; emotional, mental and physical, she creates and implements strategies to be used in the moment to begin healing processes for others. Most gatherings include hands-on activities. There's only room for results; a growth mindset. Mikkita continues to receive multiple invites to speak due this direct approach which call for peace and progress in the lives of others.

Mikkita along with her tour has scheduled and appeared for several presentations and speaking engagements, over the last 3 years with heightened interest in each state. Moving forward there will be plans to host back-to-school events, expos, workshops and conferences on healing awareness.

www.mikkitamoore.com

info@mikkitamoore.com

The Uneasy Journey

As a child I never knew my Journey to womanhood would be so uneasy......

Growing up in a home of a Strong Black Single Mother, I thought life would be great, or at least as great as it could be... Right... WRONG.

Because my mother was poor as a child, she made sure her children (especially me) would never have to "suffer" in that manner. I can remember growing up as a real latchkey kid, my mother was either at work, at school, sleep or studying. She was serious about making sure she would be financially set so that I had everything I needed, along with most of the things that I wanted. My mother made sure I was well rounded in education and life. We spent weekends at museums, art institutes, the zoo and let's not forget shopping and eating. My mother always said she wanted me to experience more than just my neighborhood. So, you can imagine my life was Great... Ha...

Growing up with a mother that was financially good, in a neighborhood that other mothers were not as financially set was not easy, I often had friends that were more like enemies, or friends that found their way to my home just to get away from their own homes. It was never genuine. Right now, I literally have NO childhood friends that I can pick up the phone and talk to today.

As a kid I spent most of my days alone and feeling as if I was never good enough to have friends. I always stood out from the crowd, rather it was the way I dressed or the way I looked to the way that my mother would take me to school and pick me up while other children had to get on the CTA bus. I can remember being teased and almost tortured just because I dressed different, while everyone was wearing named brand clothing my mother would take me to department stores like Marshall Fields, Carson's, and Dillard's to buy my clothes. Yes, I always looked nice but I never looked like my peers. My clothes weren't good enough for my peers. To them I was the poor girl that couldn't afford the name brand clothing when in fact it was the complete opposite. My mother never wanted me to look like everybody else and because of that she refused to allow me to wear what everyone else was wearing. While everyone else was being asked out to the movies or to hang out, I wouldn't be invited.

My adolescent years were absolutely horrible, because of that I started "bragging" as to how my house always had food and how my mother always took me shopping, only then is when I became "popular" kids would come over and hang out with me only because my house was the house with all the food and the cool mom that was either sleep or not home. Right now, today I don't talk to any of those people.

All of those factors molded me into wanting to be loved so bad that I would do whatever it takes to be wanted and accepted. I found myself looking for love at a very early age, trying to find real love lead me to be a mother at the age of 14 and a mother of two by the age of 16. Not by mistake but because I needed to be loved unconditionally.

Most people would say I became a woman the moment I became a mother. To that I say again… WRONG. I was just a teenage parent that had no clue who I was or who I was becoming. All I knew was hurt. After having my children, yes, I finished high school and went on to cosmetology school graduating with a 3.8 GPA and going on to do hair. By now I am a woman right... Unfortunately, that's still a NO.

After cosmetology school and having my fourth child, I opened my very first hair salon. This was the first time in life that I had ever paid bills on my own. Light bill, gas bill, the rent on the property of the salon, as well as miscellaneous bills that went along with business ownership. I had never had to pay bills at home, my mother made sure I had everything I needed and wanted. I never had to even buy diapers for my child, my mother would do that for me and call it allowance. I didn't even know what bills were until I owned my salon, I was in my 20's still thinking that money was just freely given and all you had to do was ask for it.

Fast forward….. Life for me was financially easy yet emotionally and mentally very hard. I found out through moving away to St. Louis at 37 and a lot of therapy that I was never really an adult, never paying bills, never having to truly mother my own children, never having to be anything other than a spoiled mother of 5.

Moving to St. Louis with my youngest daughter alone, I was forced to grow up and figure out life. For the first three months I lived my brother and his family to save money and be sure I had a cushion when it was time to step out of comfort into the "real" life. On October 15th, 2017, I moved into my very first home (rental, but still mine). It seems like I truly had to grow up overnight. I went from paying no household bills to having to do everything on my own. I remember calling my mother saying to her "so these things (bills) come every single month?" It seemed as if the minute I would hit the pay button, I would get an email telling me that my next bill was due.

Moving on my own, I learned what the word *mine* really meant. I also learned what the saying "do for yourself" felt like all at the same time. I was alone for the first time, with my youngest daughter, just me and her, I had very little family to lean on. Away from my mother and all the comforts of being an adult kid, I now had to be an adult, and didn't even know how.

I managed to stay afloat for the most part going to work every day, just to make sure the bills were paid on time and as in full as they could be. This was a hard taste of reality for me. It was hard to talk to my mom or go to my brother's house because I always had to act as if everything was fine and that I had it all under control, but in reality, my life was still crumbling around me, this time there was no one to come and save me.

My journey to womanhood, believe it or not is still unfolding, I am now in my 40's and I still feel as if I am all alone in this thing called life. I often battle with depression and the feelings of being overwhelmed. Truth is, I stand in this thing called life alone. I can't talk to my mom because she doesn't understand "hard times", see, she has always had a great financial life, she has never battled with depression, she has never felt alone. I can't talk to my dad because all he understands is "just go get it", he too has never battled depression or the feeling of being overwhelmed. Oh, and my brother, not sure why but he thinks I am rolling in financial blessings and that I am okay.

Now don't get me wrong, I have been happy with life as a whole for the last four and a half, almost five years now, but there are times that I have feelings of being empty, lonely and at times unwanted. However, I continue to get up every day and tell myself, that I am enough, tell myself that I will make it through this. I continue to write and prosper in *Faith* daily. I know that when I am feeling at my lowest it is because God needs me to center myself in *HIM*. I know that I need to get in my prayer corner and seek his face, seek his guidance. I truly know that life is not meant to be easy, it is meant to be purposeful... And as long as I am walking in my purpose, I know that I will be okay. I remind me self often that the bible says; Matthew 22:13-14, King James Version, *13 Then said the king to the servants, Bind him hand and foot, and take him away, and cast him into outer darkness, there shall be weeping and gnashing of teeth. 14 For many are called, but few are chosen.*

So, I am telling you, to KEEP PUSHING THROYGH… push through no matter what. Continue to love on you, like never before. If no one else loves you... YOU have to love you. Tell yourself every day that you are enough, and this too shall pass. Life is an uphill journey, just keep climbing, you can't give up, the moment you feel like you need to give up, that is the exact point the you need to PUSH harder. P.U.S.H. Pray Until Something Happens….

Chapter Two

Are We There Yet?

Laina Chelle

Laina Chelle was born in the South, but raised primarily in the Midwest. Most of her childhood was spent in several Chicagoland neighborhoods including Englewood, Pullman, and in the Western and Southern Suburbs of Chicago. A graduate of Chicago Public Schools, she furthered her education at Chicago State University as the recipient of a Presidential Scholarship. After starting a small marketing company that she wasn't quite ready to handle, she focused on retail management; working her way up from a retail sales associate to assistant manager, before switching gears to beginning a career in the Public Sector. She is a proud mother of two adult children. She also has over eight years of experience as a director of youth programs, and over four years coaching high school athletics. Her hobbies include cooking, team and shooting sports, fine arts, and spending time with family and friends. She believes in lifelong learning, and loves sharing her gifts and talents with others.

Kiya@lainachelle.com
www.lainachelle.com

Are We There Yet?

Have you ever gone on a drive without a destination? Sure, you can get behind the wheel, and hop on the road listening to your favorite soundtrack... but eventually, you've got to want to get somewhere. I began my transition to womanhood not truly knowing myself or my goals. I was on a long drive, with a full gas tank. As a high school graduate, I was unsure of what I wanted in my next phase of life. I was a people-pleaser, and I flourished whenever I was in a position to help someone behind the scenes. I've always been great at planning and organizing, and I freely share my talents and ideas with others, but I had not decided, what I wanted to do with any of my gifts for myself. I was young, naïve, and on a journey for love, trying to fill an unhealthy void. At many times, I felt like I could find someone to complete me, without the understanding that I was already whole, God doesn't make fractions.

Metaphorically, I was driving for a long time before I actually determined where I wanted to go... the road had several construction areas. The important thing is that I never ran out of gas. As a young adult, I was not financially secure. I literally worked three part-time jobs while working on my degree. I had to face several bumps and bruises along my journey. A lot of them were very hard to face, and although I don't want to repeat them, I don't regret them at all. You won't enjoy your destiny on the shortcuts! I realized in my late 20's that I was still in transition to womanhood. Although I was handling many responsibilities of an adult, including raising two children, I was still discovering my potential. After receiving my college degree, I found a good job, and I settled to focus on being a Mom. I still had not taken the time to discover what I really wanted out of life. I just focused all of my energy on being the best parent I could possibly be. But what does "being the best parent" actually look like? I came to find that the answer is very complex, and although many people do things differently, somehow, most of us generally are doing our very best at it.

I worked hard to keep my children in the same school district from elementary throughout high school, which was very different than my experience in elementary and high school. This sacrifice came at a huge cost. I struggled during the phases of motherhood for several years trying to keep up with appearances. I also struggled financially, facing pitfalls along the way due to misguided relationships and irrational decisions. I did the best thing that I thought I could do at the time, which was to become increasingly involved in a bible-based church that allowed me and my children the opportunity to see friendships and relationships in the way that God truly intended. Throughout this time, I also learned how to give back to others in several ways, including mentorship, and coaching youth sports.

There is no huge manual to life in general, but I am sure of one important fact – success leaves clues. The problem is, many people don't know where to find them, or weren't looking for them in the first place. I was keenly aware of my experiences as a teen and a young adult, and I wanted to provide a blueprint for my children that was different than the one I had. The difference between their transition to adulthood and mine comes down to one important element – Google. As a child, I would read the dictionary for fun. It was exciting for me to learn new words and phrases. But back then, I wasn't able to view different communities and cultures in the same manner as I now can with the power of the internet. The Google search engine has become my manual, blueprint, my way of learning things that we didn't focus on when I was in school, and a way to virtually see the world. To this day, I am pretty sure that people can teach themselves how to do anything if they find the right YouTube videos! I consciously seek out successful strangers on the internet that are willing to share free nuggets of knowledge, and the findings are plentiful; motivation, instruction, demonstration and feedback are right at my fingertips. I research different cultures and traditions as well, and it has truly helped me to understand the gift of tolerance. I encourage others to use the power of the internet liberally!

For years, I didn't stop to consider what I truly wanted for myself, because I was laser focused on being a support system to family and friends. I did not have an opportunity to live on my own as an adult for an extended period of time before I had children. So, a part of me still longed to have certain experiences that I simply could not afford… to travel and hang out with friends in various tropical environments, going on thrilling excursions with limitless alcoholic beverages. One day, a friend and I were discussing vacations, and I was asked, where I would want to go. I realized that I really didn't know. I didn't want the weather to be too hot, or too cold, and I didn't want to be anywhere that had several large crowds. But I definitely wanted amazing views, fresh air, peace, and incredible food. When I took a moment to really think about that, everything I really wanted was already within reach. I love nature, and I am content with a walk in the park on a sunny day, along with a meaningful conversation. As for the food, I have been known to create a masterpiece or two in my own kitchen. After taking inventory, I realized that my life is pretty fabulous as it is.

While I was in my 30's, I decided to get really REAL, and create a road map. I was well into my 30's before considering ways to create generational wealth, and leaving a legacy. I decided not to hold back on conversations about my journey, because I wanted my children to get an understanding of their lives, and how their decisions during their transition to adulthood would shape their future beyond retirement. Throughout my journey, sometimes I had to repeat some of the experiences because I didn't learn my lesson the first time! I realized that transparency is important, and discussing the experiences I faced on my journey can help our next generation. In the 90's, when Lauryn Hill sang, "Baby Girl, respect is just the minimum", I bobbed my head and sang along, but truthfully, I didn't get it at the time. Throughout my experiences, I raised my level of desire, achievement, and acceptance of myself. I raised my level of accountability and perseverance. I also raised my standards of quality people and relationships.

I am still learning to love myself unconditionally, set immovable boundaries, and achieve the very best for myself, without the need for validation or approval from others. But the learning curve is much smoother. I'm stronger, and I'm understanding the value of my health, my self-esteem, and my peace.

So, what would I tell twenty-year-old me? Don't sacrifice your life for others. **YOU OWE YOU!**

What did I learn along the journey?

1. The True Value of Time.
I understand that life is but a vapor, and the people I love the most could be here today, and gone tomorrow; so, it is important to take time to check in on the people I truly love. I have learned to place value on the time I sacrifice for others, and the time others sacrifice for me. I don't take it lightly when anyone makes time for me. As several others can attest, I have suffered great losses, but I find so much strength from the lessons I have learned through it. I realize that I owe it to myself to invest my time wisely, and that whatever time is spent on things that do not produce fruit in some area of my life is time wasted.

2. My Good is Good Enough.
I kept saying I would wait… until. I thought I should wait until I reached a level of accomplishment, without realizing

the accomplishments I have already achieved. I compared my progress to others, and sometimes got frustrated when I didn't feel like my progression was fast enough. Then one day I looked up and realized that my level of success is enough for me. I don't want to move at anyone else's pace on my journey. I am my own competition, and my toughest critic. My path is for me, and even if someone else gave me their shoes to walk a mile in, I probably wouldn't make it halfway down their lane. I'm also pretty sure that no one else would survive a day in my shoes. My journey hasn't been easy, but my strength is in my story.

3.   The Importance of Writing a Vision.
Manifestation and specificity are essential to accomplishing goals. Getting to a destination without first, having an idea of where to go makes the journey much more difficult. Imagine driving to Kentucky from New York without a GPS system, compass, or map. It's certainly still possible to get there, but you'll probably waste a lot of time along the way. I spent a lot of time not really being able to determine how to write my vision, and how to seek God and submit my plans to Him along the way. It's much easier to be prepared for the next opportunity, and develop a goal and carry out the steps along the way to complete it, than it is to daydream.

4.   Investing in Yourself Will Always Be Your Most Important Investment.
As an adult, when I listen to Whitney Houston sing, "The Greatest Love of All", every lyric has meaning that I hadn't taken the time to discover years ago. Taking the time to

study myself, and what I really love has helped me to grow essentially as a person. Doing things that make me happy has also made my contributions to others more worthwhile. I had to let go of the thought that taking the time to do things I love is selfish. I also had to learn exactly how to make myself a priority. Waiting and hoping for a magical prince (*that's at least six feet tall with a beard and knows my exact love language*) to buy me flowers and sweep me off my feet became so comical when I started regularly charming myself. Now, I buy myself flowers… because I want to… because I like them… and because I know that I deserve to have the things that make me happy!

5.   The power of saying "No".
I released the fear of saying no to others. No definitely is a complete sentence. It is perfectly okay to use it whenever applicable to express yourself. When I was younger, I was afraid to disappoint people by saying no, so I found myself in overwhelming circumstances quite often. Life became simpler and satisfying for me when I empowered myself to say no more often. Even if someone proposes a good suggestion, if the timing isn't right, it can still lead to unwanted stress. I utilized the power of my "No", and utilized my wisdom to determine when to use the power of my "Not right now". I would not have made it this far without this key element.

6.   The Power of Influence.
There is nothing like being a part of a circle of heavy hitters who don't back down from a challenge, and press towards success by any means necessary. Study the caliber of your

friends. Even as an adult, socialization rules still apply. Choosing the company that you keep definitely has an effect on your outcome, and if you're not satisfied with your current results, it's never too late to change the status quo. That doesn't mean you can't still have experiences with others who aren't as motivated. It just means, that you will probably need to be more mindful of your time with those people. Being intentional about having friends in your corner who keep pushing you to be your best, and won't be content with you in a mediocre state is an important element of many successful friendships. It is also important to understand that this level of quality may not exist in every friend, and that is okay. There are several people who have made a career of mentoring and coaching others. Seeking out experienced mentors is also a helpful tool for success.

7. Believing in Yourself is the Spark that Ignites the Fire.

The most important achievements that I have experienced all have one thing in common. At some point, I had to believe I could achieve them in order to get them accomplished. The amount of time to accomplish the objectives, and the hurdles along the way were only formalities in the journey. At times, I have put some obstacles in my own way. But, believing in myself pushed me to success in ways that no other method ever could. Believing in myself has also been the fuel to fire my passion to reach my next goal. I have been my biggest critic, but my favorite job is being my biggest fan. Manifestation cannot be achieved without affirmation.

So, what took me so long to get here…to even write about my journey?

Strength, Resilience, Endurance, and Power are traits that all African-American Women are equipped with. It's an element of our DNA – a gift from our ancestors, a part of the special blend of seasonings in our "Black Girl Magic" packet. I believe somehow, in our diligence to set higher standards, we sometimes forget to take a moment to celebrate ourselves and our accomplishments, and show others the way. Many of us are the first generation of our lineage to set and achieve success on the levels that we see now. In the realization that we are getting there, I also reached an understanding that I have a responsibility to encourage and empower as many others as I possibly can.

To quote Maya Angelou, an American poet, memoirist, and civil rights activist *(Sunrise 04/04/1928 – Sunset 05/28/2014)*, *"We delight in the beauty of the butterfly, but rarely admit the changes it has gone through to achieve that beauty."*

A truly successful person wants to leave clues. No matter how many times you read this chapter along your Journey to Womanhood, my hope is that it inspires and motivates you to celebrate who you are today, and continue to discover who you can become.

It's a Matron of Honor... Journey to Womanhood

Chapter Three

My Womanhood Experience

Latonya Willett

Latonya Brown Willett, a wife of 25 years, mother of 4, financial analyst, entrepreneur, motivational speaker, and Evangelist. Latonya was born on the Westside of Chicago. She's the next to youngest of 4 children. At a very early age, (4 years old) Latonya always had a caring heart for others. She would help others as much as she could by giving of her time, money, toys, and anything else she had to give.

As Latonya became older, she still had a caring spirit, but ran into life along the way. By the age of 15, she had her first child and by the time she was 17 she had her second child. While struggling to keep up her grades and take care of 2 children with the support of only her older sister, her second child would eventually die at the age of 4 months old on Mother's Day from SIDS. Only by the grace of God did Latonya navigate her way through depression, suicide attempts and more, to be able to care for her older son.

Four months after the death of her son, she met the man that would later become her husband. They have 2 sons together and 2 grandsons, one from the oldest and one from the middle son.

Latonya has a background in Nursing and Science. Latonya is now and has been a Financial Analyst, for the past 18 years, known as The Money Lady. She analyzes and presents budget plans, investment ideas, as well as provide insurance options. Latonya has won many awards associated with the work she does for her clients, and has been recognized and celebrated as one of the "100 Black Queens of Chicago". She's the Outreach Director of her church as well as an ordained Evangelist, has her own Non-Profit called "Blessings From Heaven". She also helps her 20-year-old son run both of his businesses, Dance Characters and BopKing Larry Entertainment. The 2 of them travel to schools teaching the children about how money works and how they can become business owner's themselves. Latonya is a real Comeback Queen with a demonstrated wealth of knowledge of life's hardships, overcoming obstacles, business, wealth creation, and legacy building.

To contact Latonya Willett, you can reach her by email at LatonyaWillett@yahoo.com

My Womanhood Experience

As a child growing up, I was very sheltered in the way that I couldn't go anywhere alone. I could only play in the backyard, and I had to be in the house once the streetlights came on. I couldn't go to anyone's house, and I especially couldn't spend the night at anyone's house. I only went to school and came home. I would occasionally go to my sister's house on the weekend as my way of escape. Even though, I was sheltered in this way, I still knew a lot of grownup things that a kid at my age should not have known.

Since my mother was the "go to" person of the family, I was exposed to a lot of things and people from all walks of life. This is why I'm so caring toward people till this day. I had family members that were drug dealers as well as drug addicts. I had family members that were pimps and prostitutes. I also had family members that were of the cloth, and family members that owned real estate and a few companies.

Me being the baby of the family, I was always right there with my mother to see the different things that transpired. By the time I was 8 years old, I knew how to stop a person from having an overdose. I knew how to protect a person having a seizure from biting their tongue. I also knew how to take care of babies, since I would always babysit for my brother and sister. Back in the day, when your mother told you not to open the door for anyone until she got back, you didn't open the door.

By the time I was 9 years old, I had been molested by a close family friend and my mother and I had started drifting apart because she found someone and was into him more than me. He wasn't very nice to any of us. I began to go to my sister's house more and more by now. While there, I met a guy named Jay that I liked. I was only 12 and he was 17. We began "dating". We just stayed outside talking every day; that is, until a year had passed. I was mad at him for some reason or another and began dating a boy that lived on the first floor. Well needless to say, Jay didn't like that very much. He picked a fight with the guy. When my sister found out, she told my mother, she told her that she should talk to me about the "birds and the bees" and to get me on birth control. My mother wouldn't hear of it, she said that I have no business doing anything, so she's not going to tell me anything. I really wasn't doing anything and had no intension of doing anything with him or anyone else. I was a virgin and was planning on staying that way. My sister pleaded with my mother to just do it as a safety precaution so that if I did slip up and have sex, I would be protected.

Well, the time finally came when I felt like I could take the leap. I was a straight A student, but still didn't know anything about sex. I trusted him with everything. He told me he would "pull out". When my mother said that she wasn't going to let me go to my sister's house anymore, he panicked. He had his aunt to call my mother and tell her how much he loved me and that he was trying to get me pregnant so that we could be together. I was horrified, devastated and anything else you can think of. You can imagine how that night went.

Now, I'm 14 years old and pregnant in the eighth grade. No one in my class really knew because I wasn't showing yet. I didn't start showing until I was a freshman in high school. I hid it for a while. My stomach was so flat that when it began to get big, it just looked like a regular size stomach. I would later have to go to Simpson which was a school for pregnant girls. I saw a lot there as well. There were girls there that had the same baby daddy. When they found out, they would fight each other instead of him. I never understood that.

Fast forward to my Junior year of high school. I'm pregnant again. I hid this pregnancy as well because I knew my mother would want me to have an abortion. By this time, I was going to school during the day and going to work at the nursing home in the afternoon and weekends for our nursing work program. I had also gotten a job working at McDonald's. I was determined to take care of my baby.

Once my baby, DeAndre came, (another boy) I would have a bookbag full of books on one arm, a one-and-a-half-year-old on my hip, a baby bag on the other arm, and a baby carrier with the baby inside in the other hand. I would pick them up from my downstairs neighbor who kept them for me from time to time, and I would go to my sister's house a few blocks away to do homework, take care of my babies, babysit her children and help them with their homework while she was at work. Later, her hours would change to the point where she would be able to keep my babies for me while I was in school, as well as my father when he moved in with her. This made things much easier.

At this point everything was going as good as good can be. I was going to school, I was working, taking care of my babies, with my sister and my daddy's help. Until, one day, Mother's Day to be exact, at 5am my father was waking me up saying that he thinks something is wrong with the baby because he never sleeps that long. DeAndre was our rooster. You could put him to sleep at 4:45 am and he would be right back up at 5am every morning, like clockwork. I tried to say there was nothing wrong, that he was just tired, but deep down I knew. My father picked him up and tried to wake him, but he would never wake again. This was my journey to womanhood.

I went through a lot of counseling after that. I even had to take pills for depression. Four months later, I would eventually meet the man that is now my husband. We have 2 beautiful boys' together. It seems as if that's the only gender I can produce, lol. He's really helped me get through a lot; he came at the time when I was in the depths of the depression. Through much prayer and support from my family I was able to get through.

It's a Matron of Honor... Journey to Womanhood

Chapter Four

Young and UnSullied

Cutrina Oliver

Poet, accomplished realtor, and minister **Cutrina Oliver** is making her debut as a published writer. She fell in love with and began writing while still in elementary school. Ms. Oliver is also a mother of four and has two grandchildren. She is a sibling with three older brothers and a younger sister. She enjoys writing, travel, fashion, mentoring the youth and spending time with family, Ms. Oliver looks forward to writing many more books, reading often, and continuing to development of her interests and skills.

You can visit her online at WEBSITE cutrinao.com or on Instagram (@)."#mscmo1

Young and Unsullied

The Pursuit

My coming of age didn't come naturally, I forced it on myself… Let me explain; see growing up I was considered a little fast-tail lil girl that was going to just have a bunch of babies and do nothing with my life. Well, my critics were partially right, it all started when I went to live with my aunt and uncle. My mom worked at night as a custodian, so there was no supervision for me my brothers, which were teenagers doing their own thing. Now, back to when everything changed, I started living with my aunt, uncle and their teenage son, it was in the summer of '83 my body was developing, what the old people would say I was filling out, but I was just like all of the other little girl's in the neighborhood, trying to be cute for the little boys to notice us. There was this one boy I liked, let's call him "Timothy", we would all meet on my block, play games together; like hide and seek or should I say hide and get, hahaha. While playing one day, Timothy and I, hid together and couldn't be found. He told me he liked me, we kissed and everybody start calling us boyfriend and girlfriend. We did have a crush on each other but it didn't progress any further than that kiss. We all continued to meet up and play throughout the summer. Soon the weather started to change, it was back to school before we knew it.

There was this one day when things took a swift turn; I was running late for school, I had over slept. My uncle was outside wiping on his car, his friend was there, they were chopping it up, that's what it's called when men folk are hanging outside talking, I asked my uncle if he would drop me off at school he said yes and for me to go get my stuff. As I was walking in the house his friend Marcus said, man I can drop her off I'm going that way, my uncle then says to me "hurry up Marcus is going to take you to school". I got my backpack came outside to leave. He said the door is open, he drove a black 68 Chevy Impala, fixed all up with loud pipes and the interior was an off white, it was just as clean inside as the black shined on the outside. The car smelled as good as he looked. As we were driving, he says "what grade are you in?" I responded I'm a sophomore, he said what's that 10th grade, I said yes then he said I know you got a little boyfriend that's why you looking all good. I blushed and said no I don't have a boyfriend, I just like looking cute, he smiled and grasped his hand over mine on the seat. I was scared to move it so he had his hand over mine the entire ride.

Once we got to the school, I said you can drop me off outside the gate but instead he drove to the drop-off area, pulled in front of the administration office, before I got out of the car he pulled out a wad of money, at first he took out a 100 dollar bill so he counted out five 20 dollar bills and said that's for lunch. I took the money said thank you but mind you my uncle gives me 10 dollars every morning for lunch. When I turned to get out of the car, what he did next totally caught me off guard, he grabbed me by the chin with his thumb and index finger, turned my face toward his and kissed me on the lips. I remember his lips were nice and soft, when the kiss ended, he told me to have a good day and that he would talk to me later. I got out of the car in a daze like what just happened? I hurried into the administration office to get a late pass and went about my day.

The Romance

The toying with me went off and on throughout the school year. Soon the summer of '84 was coming, which is when things really got interesting. One evening I was home alone, Marcus came by looking for my uncle, I explained that no one was home but me. He asked me to take a ride with him and said he would bring me right back before anybody gets home, so I locked up the house and got in the car with him. He stopped at a liquor store just down the way, bought a pint of Hennessey and a 16oz bottle of Coke. He also had two cups of ice, when he got back in the car, he poured one cup straight Hennessey, the second cup he poured half Coke and half Hennessey, he then says the half and half cup is yours, and told me to take a drink. He said take it slow until you get used to it. I was feeling a little buzzed, he drank his cup straight down. He turns to me and says we gotta get you used to drinking, then you'll be able to drink it straight like me, he laughed continued drive. He turned into an alley way, behind these apartments, pulled into the parking space, turned off the car and said let's go inside. He said this was one of his little spots, it was nice and clean, wreaked of men's cologne. We walked into the living room, he motioned me to sit down and to make myself at home. I sat down, put the cups on the table, he sat right next to me, there was no room between us. He was smelling all good, he leaned over, looked in my eyes and kissed me, it was a long-wet kiss. His lips were soft, when we stopped kissing, he would call me his "young thang". In my mind, I was like he really likes me! We sat on the sofa with his back to me he laid across my chest and I put my arms around him. We talked about us getting to know each other better and spending time together. It then got quiet and still, he sat up, reached his hand back for my hand, I folded my fingers around his, and he led me to the bedroom. I was a puzzle and he enjoyed every piece of me. I had never been kissed all over before, when the slow dance had ended, I felt so drained but alive all at the same time. We laid there in silence with my head on his chest, I looked up at him, we kissed then I motioned to get up, he stopped me and said I got you, as if to say he knew we had conceived.

As we were leaving, he asked if I was okay with what had happened, I answered yes. He gave me the key to the apartment and said whenever I wanted to come over to be with him or just get away for a while, I could at any time. At first, I was looked at him like are you sure and he said I told you I got you. He drove me home, and as Marcus drove off, my cousin was driving up. He said, were you with him, at first, I denied it, but then I told him that I was. He simply said be careful if my uncle, which is his dad finds out there might be a problem.

The Aftermath

By this time, I was spending as much time as I could with Marcus. We were careful not to get caught but I started getting sick and couldn't keep anything down. I hadn't had my period for about two months, my clothes were still fitting so I was like I'm not pregnant. I've always had irregular periods, so I didn't think anything of it. One day Marcus came over, but my uncle, aunt, my cousin and I were headed to the mall, as I was walking out the house, he was coming in, he hit me on the butt, no one saw it. He then says, baby you look different, I said what do you mean, he said we'll talk later. I called him that evening, we had a secret code when we called each other, he asked me had I been having my period, and at first, I hesitated, then I said, why did you ask me that, he said I think you might be pregnant. At this point, I let him know it had been almost two months since I had my last period. He said, if you are pregnant what do you want to do, I said I didn't know. He then told me that I could abort the baby, so I caught the bus, went to Planned Parenthood, took a pregnancy test and I was indeed pregnant. I called him, he picked me up from the doctor's office. I cried all the way home, I told him that the Doctor said the only way I could have an abortion, was to go to California, they would do pregnancy terminations up to 6 months.

We were planning to see how we could go there to have it done. He would pay for everything. I listened to him talk about what he wanted, but then I asked him to stop somewhere so that we could talk. I said to him, you never asked me what I wanted to do, he said, you are right, but you are so young, I know you don't want no baby. I said, yes, I do I want my baby, if you don't want to be around, I don't care. Did I mention that he had a woman, and his woman had just had a baby! He said, if you want the baby, I will be there for you and the baby. That turned out to be a lie, because once my mom got wind of it, I had to move back home. I couldn't see him anymore she threatened to have him locked up for statutory rape. I went home, raised my daughter with the help of my family and never saw her dad again, maybe once or twice in passing, but never where we could talk. Him and my uncle were no longer friends, once it came out that he was the father, they actually had a falling out over it. So needless to say, there were a few lives changed because of our secret rendezvous of the adult kind. However, I would not change anything in the world, because the Aftermath was my beautiful daughter. Besides the very way he made a life for himself, me and his other women also became his demise you know what they say don't get high off your own supply.

That was my Journey to Womanhood... It's not every one's story but it is the story that has made me The Woman that I am Today!!!!!

Chapter Five

A New Beginning

Meighan J. Cole

Meighan Cole have run and owned a Transportation Logistics business since late 2012, coming together during a pandemic in 2020 with her sister & family to run a food truck DUO "MaMaw's Kitchen" serving the best Italian beefs, funnel cakes & Chicken in town with recipe's inspired from her late mother Andrea Cole. Wholistically Living an online store geared toward wholistic living & more. Wholisticwayz.com

Cited as an influential woman in the transportation industry via news articles "the Voice Aurora" "Aurora School District 129" "Yorkville School District 115" "Tell Me Something Good Magazine" for outstanding service and ethical practices in the Illinois Aurora/Yorkville/Oswego area, SBDC black business owner spot light article 2020.

Meighan a small business owner, motivational speaker, author and empowerment coach. Author "Juicing For Life E-Book" & Organizer of Juicing for Life Empowerment group via Facebook" Meighan has also been featured as a Winning Woman via "She Wins Society Sisterhood Group with Andromeda Raheem, Transformation Wednesdays blog post with Chamar Logan, several podcast shows Empower Me with Purpose Network and the Lucas Live Show!

A pioneer in the transportation industry making her mark as a "systemprenuer" "Meighan says I came up in the late 80s as a foster child. My only goal in life was to beat the odds and the system that was meant to take me away from everything I knew and to destroy my family. There were several strikes against me it was a must to surpass them and not let them get the best of me. I went from being a high school dropout to finally getting a HS Diploma via homeschool, taking 4years to obtain a college degree. I have worked very hard and remained humble during the process because I personally know the struggle. Life is never a race you will get there in Gods time. I own my title from "Foster Care to CEO". CEO, is not in a Corporate sense it merely means that you are the CEO of your own life, your own destiny and the only person that can stop you is you".

I believe all things & people are Beautiful!

Life is full of inspirational moments I always say the good, bad or indifferent.

"I, like so many of us, have encountered many obstacles in life. Those obstacles were soon reminders for me to become the change I wanted to see in the world".

Social Media Follow:

IG Personal Blog MeighanCole_businessacumen

IG Food Truck MaMawsKitchen1

Facebook: Meighan Cole

Website: Meighancole.com

A New Beginning

The Beginning

I was your glass slipper, plastic heel, and hop scotch playing little girl! My momma kept me dressed in some of the hottest fashion for an 80s baby! I just wanted to play with the kids on the block; living in the pretty little yellow house on Jackson St in my birth town Joliet IL. Going from granny Georgia house on Grant St. to granny Precious house on Benton St. raised with a lot of cousins we were always in the kitchen learning some of the best home cooked recipes from Auntie Sarah.

The Dreamer

I've always been a big dreamer since the age of 5. Often times day dreaming quietly playing with my cabbage patch dolls or my easy bake oven, those two were my best friend. I dreamed about being a lawyer, a cook, a beautician. I knew I was going to be somebody someday at a very young age. The oldest of 9 siblings the responsible one "HA" wondering why life at age 5 felt like a rush? Why was I wearing the hat of an adult at such a young age?

All I wanted to do was be a kid, but instead I was busy being little MOMMA. Ivan don't do this, Wryan don't do that. The boy's, the two born after me, we were stair steps as the old folks would say. Being left alone to baby sit what was a 5-year-old to do? Why on heavens green earth at 5 couldn't I just play with my easy bake oven, my dolls, and my friend's? What I didn't see coming was eventually

56

being a Sis/Momma for real raising my youngest sibling after granny Georgia had a stroke in 2007. "I laugh now at how life comes back around full circle."

Girl 8

At eight years old, I remember like it was yesterday. The day came where we were stripped from everything and everybody, we knew our FAMILY. 5 children by my mother, 3 boys, 2 girls; 4 of us being placed in foster care 3 of us together, 1 separated and 1 getting to stay with their grandma. Talking about being 8 and confused, well I wouldn't quite say confused. I was actually very smart at that age I learned young about the gift of discernment.

I didn't know what it was to know something or to have a feeling about something and then to actually be dead on the spot right about it. I learned later in life that discernment is a gift! I knew that something wasn't right; Girl 8 was very curious, nosey and determined to solve the mystery of being taken away from my entire family & the why. I had to quickly unlearn my entire being and immediately learn merely how to survive. I remember my grandmother Georgia screaming crying as the DCFS removed us one by one from her arms. I remember them telling her if she hid us one more day that she would go to jail for kidnapping. The devastating look on my grandmother's face was pain, agony; she was torn when she had to relinquish her rights. If it was left up to Georgia Lynn it would've been her and 8 grandchildren piled up in her 2 bedroom motel apartment.

Girl 8 had a lot to say in the moments of being stripped away from her family. I wanted to know why and at that very moment my voice was stripped when I asked. I was not heard and surely my bright light and smile weren't so bright anymore; it hurt to smile. I went from smiling to the numb face of being misunderstood. Fighting to be heard from one foster home to another because of the mistreatment toward my siblings, being separated from them in the same home. I was the foster parent's favorite little girl, "I guess", often times taken into the room being fondled by the foster parents' relatives/children. I couldn't take it anymore I grew up thinking something was wrong with me. The molestation started in my very own family first before being removed. I wondered what was the purpose of moving us if the same cycle was going to take place. I grew up questioning myself, why me? Sitting quietly and timid I knew the cycle had to end. When they couldn't control me for talking and telling so much, they made me change my self- image. They force me into a good ole Jerry curl. I couldn't understand why I needed a curl; my hair was down my back I couldn't stand that wet hair LOL. My rebellion and resentment for foster care & the entire system grew stronger. I said from that point on I was going to give the system "*HELL*" until they sent me back home. Finally placed at age 9.5 with my grandparents in Maywood Il.

The Separation

I was separated from my siblings because I wouldn't shut up, *"remember I said I wanted to be a lawyer hahaha."* I remember the caseworker telling every home she placed me in, that I was too bossy and I was always trying to be somebody's momma.

She wasn't concerned about what happened to us or me for that matter she was more concerned about placement and I mean fast placement to go on about her day to day. She didn't mind diminishing my precious character, making all of the foster homes think I had a problem. Well, actually I did. It was bottled up rejection, anxiety, resentment, feeling unloved all wrapped up in one little girl. I needed help and I was reaching, but often times not heard.

One heck of a caseworker she was "implies sad face". I tell you, I chuckle at her now because, by no means was I going to back down to her or anyone else who thought they could mistreat me and my siblings. As long as I had a voice I was not backing down, "I was very territorial over my siblings being the oldest. I had seen far too much foolishness growing up way too fast. My favorite saying is "I had to fight all my life" Oprah Winfrey Color Purple.

Seventeen & Grown a HAWT Mess

I just wanted to go home back to my hometown just one more time. J-Town is what they called it, I wanted to see what I was missing. Finding it hard to connect with my roots, I stumbled, I fell hard into a trap of wanting to fit it, to be seen as bout it- bout it. A high-school dropout trying to figure it out. I get a little weed, I'd sell it, I see the fly clothes, I'd steal them, oh boy what path was I headed down? I wanted to be down like never before, hanging with a boyfriend who sold dope a gun was put to my head. Even still no matter the cause or whom I hurt I wanted to be about that life. I was living foul and I was the biggest flunky ever, for a long time, but when I caught on I moved on.

Everything seemed to go wrong living pillar to post, sleeping from couch to couch, floor to floor. I met a couple of good friend's along the way whom opened their doors; for that I am forever grateful. Let me make it very clear though, it didn't have to be this way! My granddad Jesse and G-ma Cheryl doors were always opened, BUT remember I said I was rebellious. My PRIDE! My G-dad was a protector, he was too strict and I did not like that, I rebelled for a long time. Getting tired of myself at just 17 years old I grabbed a good job, a car and I got my very first apartment. I remember my assertiveness and my wittiness. I told the apartment manager, "look, I know I am only 17, but I promise I will be your best tenant and I will not cause you any problems." She was reluctant, but she made a phone call, ran my credit and said her dad said yes! I was capable, the rent was $475, thank God for $475 rent, plus my G-ma was not going to let me struggle. Still a ward of the state, independent living at its finest, I begin to pave my own lane and stay there. I finally had a place to call my very own home. I had one last issue; I didn't have a high school diploma. I am landing good jobs but my education was not secured, then bam! I get terminated because I lied on my application about having a high school diploma.

I recited this quote daily *"you may encounter many defeats, but you may not be defeated. Because it may be necessary to encounter the defeats, so you can know who you are, what you can rise from and how you can still come out of it"*.

I worked like a hound from 17 years old forward, still making some mistakes and stumbling through the rat race. Fast forward, 19, I get caught stealing, for sure that part of my life was not my ministry LOL. I thank GOD for the woman who spoke life over me I lived with her prior to getting my own apartment, she hugged me and told me, she seen Greatness in me and that stealing was not for me, GOD rest her soul. Even the store clerk that caught me, never called the police on me, she made me walk the items back to her store and said you're better this now GO and go home. I gave her the hardest time ever, but she kept her promise and her word, what that meant then, means so much more now at almost 40, I get it and understand it. No jail time or felonies faced that would have been a never-ending generational curse that lived on.

At this point, I was tired of myself, confused and needed change asap, I was not going to be a statistic I was determined to break the cycle. I began my research and was determined to get my high school diploma; I found an online program. I had 4 classes left, I struggled in Algebra, I felt stupid, I cried. I called out to a family member, one of my favorite cousins, whom helped me pull through in algebra. I graduated with a 3.4 GPA! I learned the art of asking for help at that time was very important in life.

"The Art of Letting Go"

I was raised in an era where generational curses ran deep and were normalized until I was placed with my grandparent's; I remember my G-Ma pouring words of affirmations and wisdom into me and she would say, "You show them and I mean you beat the odds and don't worry about what people think or say about you." Being schooled by G-ma was always intriguing, because she made me feel like the prettiest and smartest little girl in the world. I could've held onto everything that happened to me, but it would not have served me well throughout life. Her words stayed upfront in my mind and the prayers of granny Jeanette stayed in my heart; Psalms 91.

At the young precious age of 10 I learned about therapy, group counseling, and family counseling because I told my G-dad and G-ma that I hated my mother. My grandma was committed to making sure I was whole; therefore, therapy was enforced.

Growing and glowing through what I went through, understanding that it certainly was not my fault nor our mothers' fault is when my journey to womanhood began. When I accepted perfect peace and understanding it changed my life forever.

Ding! It clicked, I learned that sometimes you have to be willing to feel the pain, allow the emotions to flow through you and GO through the process. "There is something about feelings; they are informational, they let us know, if we are loving or abandoning ourselves". There were a lot of times I was doing just that; abandoning my very own well- being.

On my journey to womanhood I discovered something, I discovered that it is OK to feel. I took some time to inner bond with myself and to align my intentions. I forgave myself for the things I had done, events that transpired and what I allowed to happen. I gave myself the grace and time to heal, to fall in love with me again.

Journeying to Womanhood has been no easy task, but when I let go of all of the false beliefs, resentment, bitterness, insecurities, the pain, failed relationships, heart breaks, childhood trauma, sibling rivalry, mother/daughter trauma, black sheep (rejection); I then learned the art of letting go. Letting go, to live in the overflow to freedom, joy, happiness and abundance.

I was my own worst enemy and critic; 'I was TOXIC'. Although, I was told that I was beautiful, there were times I didn't feel that way. I hardly believed it, there was just too much pain at 31, I showed up to the bathroom mirror again. I remember having a deep conversation with myself literally talking to myself and replying "I laugh now". I told myself, "Meighan get off your pity pot and wake up to who you are and what GOD has called you to be". At that time, I began to affirm myself, I told myself; I AM not my childhood pain, I AM not the black sheep, I AM not rejected, I AM not insecure I AM NOT... I AM NOT... I AM NOT. I began to affirm I AM loved, I AM free, I AM bold, and I AM confident most of all I AM

BEAUTIFUL, "we will talk about this in my next book" I literally hated the word beautiful.

I changed my thoughts, and from there my words and actions followed suit. I began to affirm my entire life; I began to speak life again to everyone and everything around me. Somewhere on my journey I lost sight, and I needed clarity, I was eager to get it by any means necessary. I promised myself to never dim my light again or to fall into agreement with values that were not true. I went back to my roots I pulled out the wholistic manual and I began to indulge! I wanted a whole, happy and free life. I affirmed change, I then created the space and time to educate myself and do so!

During my journey, I realized that the rejection, my insecurities, my aspirations to live again freely and whole, strengthened me. I learned that it was important to cut off the noises from the world and to get clear about my heart's desires; it was scary, but it was worth it. In this season I learned that my soul needed rest. I learned here, that rest is a gift and a command. I became open to being vulnerable and letting go of what I could not control. Being a control freak was not the answer anymore, I had to relinquish control and that did not feel good! I knew that losing control would require determination and transformation from within, because I knew how to steer this boat. I had to process it all and give myself a time out. I learned that doing less, potentially yielded higher results. Moving out of my comfort zone was surely a game changer, ditching expectations and living my own best life!

FORGIVENESS is Key: I pray this helps another woman on her Journey

I asked GOD to forgive me so that I could forgive others. Forgiveness was my greatest breakthrough. I told GOD, I was no longer the victim and that I was the VICTOR. I started walking upright in forgiveness, I remember going around saying I forgive you; I forgive me, it became a daily habit for me to recite. People began to say "Meighan you're glowing again." I posted reminders all over my bathroom mirrors, quotes and affirmations to remind me that each day was a new day to wake up and forgive like never before. I bowed out of thrashing other's with hateful words, I bowed out of having the need to be right, I bowed out of wanting to fit in. I bowed out, because I knew the damage it could have and the lifetime it could take to repair.

I knew forgiveness and finding peace; obtaining Freedom was truly the key to unlock your Happiness and Blessings.

My Goal in life is to empower others to obtain freedom and my only hope is that my story reaches and inspires just one person!

I AM Divinity, I AM not broken, I do not need fixing, I AM perfect the way I am! I AM Light!

I AM Forgiven, I AM Peace, I Deserve to Live Life Abundantly and Freely! The life you want to live is the Life you have to be willing to create.

It's a Matron of Honor... Journey to Womanhood

Chapter Six

Clothed with Goodness

Q.R. Williams-Oakes

Q.R. Williams-Oakes is a passionate writer who explores expressing written word in all genres. In 2019, she solidified being the owner of Epiphany Expression LLC; a small business with a global vision that assists with creative writing and notary services. She is currently the Senior Administrative Assistant to the COO and CEO of Southland Care Coordination Partners, Inc; which is a company that assist health plans and serves the community. She is certified as a Community Health Worker and Mental Health First Aid Advocate. She recently obtained certification in Restorative Justice 101. Q.R. is a constant supporter of social services. She is also the co-author of the book, 'After We Parted: Rebuilding Our Lives After Divorce'.

She is a divorcee after 16 years of marriage and have a teenage son, John who is the co-author of the book 'Teen Talk: Embracing One's Identity In Today's Times'.

Q.R. wants you to know that she prays your journey is one of great insight and joy.

Her motto is "I lived it; I learned from it... I don't regret it. Now, I write about it."

Epiphany Expression LLC

epiphanyexpression@gmail.com

Clothed with Goodness

When you are the matron of honor, you are normally asked to wear a certain garment. It may resemble the others, but something unique normally accompanies it.

Not only the clothing, but the heart should be one that reflects a badge of honor. This is one of the closest relationships to the bride and certain responsibilities should be carried; it's more than carrying the fragrance of flowers. This position is reserved for an armor bearer; an act of service physically and spiritually. A personal assistant designated for the special day. A participant who is willing to walk to the front lines of battle for you. Their job is to make sure you are prepped and ready to make those steps down the aisle. A short visual walk that marks the beginning of a new journey in the natural world. A path that you can't be for certain the distance but, the desire should be an infinite road; until time stands still and life stops.

Go beyond the bridal journey and think about your life's journey in its entirety. Look in the mirror; take a detailed look at every feature and flaw. That image you see gazing back at you is truly your matron of honor on this side of the journey. Don't ever view her through broken glass; It will distort your perception of her. Do more than glance at her, from a clear view. Will she care for you? Will she love and support you in every decision; despite the feelings or results? Will she not give up on you and encourage you daily? Will her words be ones of affirmation or destruction? Will she provide you with peace or torment? Will she help protect your heart or will she attempt to defeat you with your own weaponry bag? In times of spiritual warfare will she pray for you gracefully, casting down evil principalities or will she usher in demonic spirits into your life? Your soul, your complete make-up reflects your life's internal matron of honor. How will you treat her? How will you walk with her? Please don't stand in her way. Break bread with her; Pour from a new wineskin into her cup. Allow there to be an overflow of goodness.

Will she sway to the beat of your purpose and destiny? Will she be a hindrance and a roadblock in your life? Will she help you maneuver around sighted challenges or will she throw more obstacles in your path? Will she be a guide and respected companion? Will she cause you to pause and reset the navigation system? Or will she have you come to a complete halt, stuck in the middle of the madness with no apparent way out? Can you trust her detours and re-routing? Will she have you lost with no point of reference? Can she help you arrive at your designation carrying joy, divine order and legacy? You need her present, focus and active more than anything else in this world. Please bond with her and allow her to shift accordingly; to help you evolve into the very being you were created to be. Rose petals have been laid before you to walk on. Allow your steps to have order. She should help lift you up whenever needed. Walk with vision towards your life's mission my dear.

Those first steps that any of us take can be wobbling but puts us in a position of motion. We're moving, despite fears and present level of confidence. In the spirit, I believe we are reaching out for the Father as we desperately want to get closer to purpose. He is reaching towards us as well (Psalm 136:12). If you feel like you are lagging behind in your journey, you can definitely catch up. Keep moving at your own pace. Perhaps you are being led by the Spirit; not being behind at all. Yes, your faith walk may not resemble others. God won't intervene during every moment; we have to just experience certain things for character development. He has to show us who we are, for He already knows. This all prepares us to inhabit the ability to continuously propel forward. God wants to help take us to the next level of our journey.

Dressing appropriately for the weather conditions or occasion is vital. Wearing the right garment enables you to freely physically move while adapting to your environment. In command or ranking, your garment tells your position and may reveal your title. Our spiritual garment is 'Our Comforter' (John 14:16). God allows us to partake and carry His wisdom. We are a reflection of Him. We are His garment. We carry His Word and our actions should be in direct response to it. Now I understand more why the elders or ancestors refer to a woman's husband as "her garment". He should be her covering, her protector. We have that in our Abba; He is the ultimate covering.

There have been examples of the journey of womanhood since the beginning of time, especially biblically. Let's start with Eve; we owe her a tremendous amount of gratitude, but so much of our pains stem from the root of her. She was a woman who had to travel outside of perfect peace after encountering a brief interruption within that; She had to endure long suffering because of one decision. She still helped raise a nation, generation after generation. If "Oops, I did not mean to do it" was a person, it would be her. Many parables outline a journey or pilgrimage of womanhood: Jael, Hannah, Prophetess Deborah, Ruth and Naomi.

Growing up playing with a yellow, white and blue plastic kitchenette, that sat across from a large twin size wooden bed. Hand crocheted rugs laid over brown rugged carpet, that my mother made to help make my quaint living space have that extra touch. Before that point I was my mother's personal doll baby. On any given Sunday wearing bonnets and furs. My older sister teased me saying I resembled a character from 'Dynasty'. Now, I was becoming a little lady, playing with my dolls, big and small. I was going to be the best mother I could be to them; it didn't even cross my mind at the time that most of them didn't even resemble me within their miniature marketing appearance. I was gentle but rough; playful but yet so serious about life. Such a loner but interacted so well with others. I created my own world on so many levels. A place of creativity, fantasy and wonder. A hyper imagination, while daydreaming constantly carried me through each day.

Down the road as I approached my teenage years my mother prepared me in advance; teaching me more about hygiene and menstrual cycles. I already had a bag of maxi pads in my chestier drawer, for when the moment arrived. The first one I unwrapped and placed in a tub that was filled with one-third water; experimenting to see if the commercials were right. How much moisture could it absorb? Will my cotton boat float? I probably would have gotten popped really good if my mother knew I was playing with a new pad; that was not considered a cheap feminine product to buy.

An older lady (well she was older compared to me) advice was, "Look at it before you give it away". That moment stood out to me then and now. A lot of women have been laying with a man for so long or have been associated with several men without knowing what it is that they are giving away. They haven't even seen one of the best parts of them and allowed someone else to explore it. She told me to get a mirror and look at it for myself. When I returned home, I nervously took a look and one of the physical parts of my anatomy that allows me to be in the community of women. This was like a gender reveal. I knew what I would find, but how would I react to its appearance? Looking down at it is far different than seeing your vulva as a whole. A small part of me but I want to recognize as much as I can about myself, physically and spiritually. Unbeknownst to me, this would give me more of the comfort to look at myself in a full-length mirror. Outwardly beautiful in every way. Even on days that I didn't recognize it; On those days when I just didn't see a desired image in the mirror's frame. A contrast of satisfaction and disgust.

I know I am discussing a lot about my feelings growing up but that is due to childhood being so pivotal in our upbringing and life's experiences; along with transitioning into adulthood… womanhood. So many women can't fully mature or heal after dealing with childhood emotions and trauma. You have to give attention to the little girl in order to nourish the woman. The woman can't grow if the child is still starving.

I had to get comfortable enough with me. I needed to get to the place of being free; emerging from the cocoon. All of who I was seemed very much apparent to me. With a shield up so I could continue to have my private dwelling. In my mind my entire childhood prepared me for womanhood. I was a reliable babysitter and nurturer. I watched how my parents interacted and handled business. I picked through my mental garden, plucking out weeds and anything I didn't want in my life. I was domesticated and willing to invest my all in a marriage; along with family life. I knew by caring for everybody else's children; I was preparing for motherhood. I started working quite young in my life and began to understand more about taxes and savings. I knew in my heart the transition into womanhood would be smooth. I was already equipped to perform all tasks required of me. I still wasn't fully ready to deal with the emotions and reactions that would come with that. Being quiet during so many situations; How do I carry my voice in an appropriate way and be respectfully heard?

Now showing emotions; how can I refrain from being overly sensitive? Now, I could see I required work to become a better me. Normally having all the answers, being so self-assured. Now, how do I vocalize and react like a mature woman should? How do I decipher when to hold my tongue, when I was silent for so long? Extremely honest with a huge filter; how do I not regret the power that I allow to roll off my lips? The emotions and heart of a woman was something that caused some discomfort. Maturity should come with age and wisdom should surely follow.

The brain fully matures at twenty-five and I could feel the difference. The way I asset, processed and utilized information weren't exactly the same. I began to care less and less about perception and reputation. There is freedom looking at me through my own eyes; instead of the eyes of others. I wanted to be transparent in my current stands and asked God to reveal the way He sees me. I had to speak life upon my life. I had to be okay during times I didn't have all the answers. Humble enough to acquire what was not in my possession. I had to learn not to carry the spirit of shame or rejection. I had to let go of thoughts of potentially being embarrassed or betrayed. I am careful regarding the spirit of pride. Not being full of myself, but being filled with good things and learning to take it all in; enjoying the moment. I know when I stumble; I will recover. I had to seek God more and hear His voice clearly. All of this dealt with matters of the heart and the healing that was needed. Healing and revival go hand and hand. The spirit needs a constant refresher.

I had to consult with wise women, so I could learn from their experiences. Learning to be careful not to embrace bad advice with good intentions. I continuously became comfortable in my own skin. I am smiling in abundance now; I am embracing me. I am open to receiving love. Laughter is truly medicine and I can be found laughing from my soul. As time goes on; I understand more of the things I once questioned. Everything meant for me I will receive it. I have already made room for it. Now reaching that 35th year mark, seeing how those additional years of growth were needed and how it influenced me to be the person I am today. Joy covers me daily. I am different in the best way. I am looking forward to seeing what comes with age and the added years of exploration that will be upon me. Womanhood is arriving to the place of knowing who you are and where you are destined to go.

Our essence is our aura, the presence of what is in our heart and soul. I always wanted to do the right things and for the most part that came easy. I believe so many moments as a little girl helped cultivate how I saw life and helped me get to the place of knowing me and loving me in my adulthood. I am thankful for the imprints I see behind me and I am looking forward to the steps in front of me.

It's easy to follow God when He is giving you what you want and telling you what you want to hear. What about those moments when God's instructions go against your plans? It isn't always easy to do what you don't desire but trust God's path. Don't waiver off that path. You never want to wander outside of the Will of God.

May your heart always seek the Lord. May you be forever faithful to the promises you made to your life's matron of honor. May your journey be blessed with good health, continuous wealth and godly wisdom; maintaining a magnificent view. Don't go backwards; cover yourself by being clothed in the right garment. We all have mountains to climb; you don't want to be the cause of you having to suffer through more. I pray you have unspeakable joy and laugh with great freedom. You are extraordinary and glorious. You are the apple of God's eye; His unique artwork and the ultimate masterpiece. Everything you do won't be right or perhaps fair; allow your harvest to be plentiful with good fruits because of the righteous seeds you planted. May your essence carry you through seasons of liberty and forever remain within your legacy. May your spirit wear a sash of godly love and a victorious crown. Step forward and step up my sister.

It's a Matron of Honor... Journey to Womanhood

Conclusion

Thank you for taking the time to read "It's a Matron of Honor, The Journey to Womanhood"

In this anthology, we the Authors, wanted to share our story of our journey to womanhood to be able to help you in whatever journey stage that you may be in. Remember you can and will get through this.

The bible says in Isaiah 40:31 "But they who wait for the Lord shall renew their strength; they shall mount up with wings like eagles; they shall run and not be weary; they shall walk and not faint." I ask that you hold on, hold on to your faith, do not faint, your waiting is not in vain.

Remember that your prayers are being heard. You have to continue to love on you, continue to heal and grow into yourself, continue to have faith in knowing that God is working on your behalf. It will all work out in due time, in due season, and all in God's timing....

Thank you!

Invisible Daughter LLC

Under the umbrella of Mikkita Moore LLC

www.mikkitamoore.com

It's a Matron of Honor... Journey to Womanhood

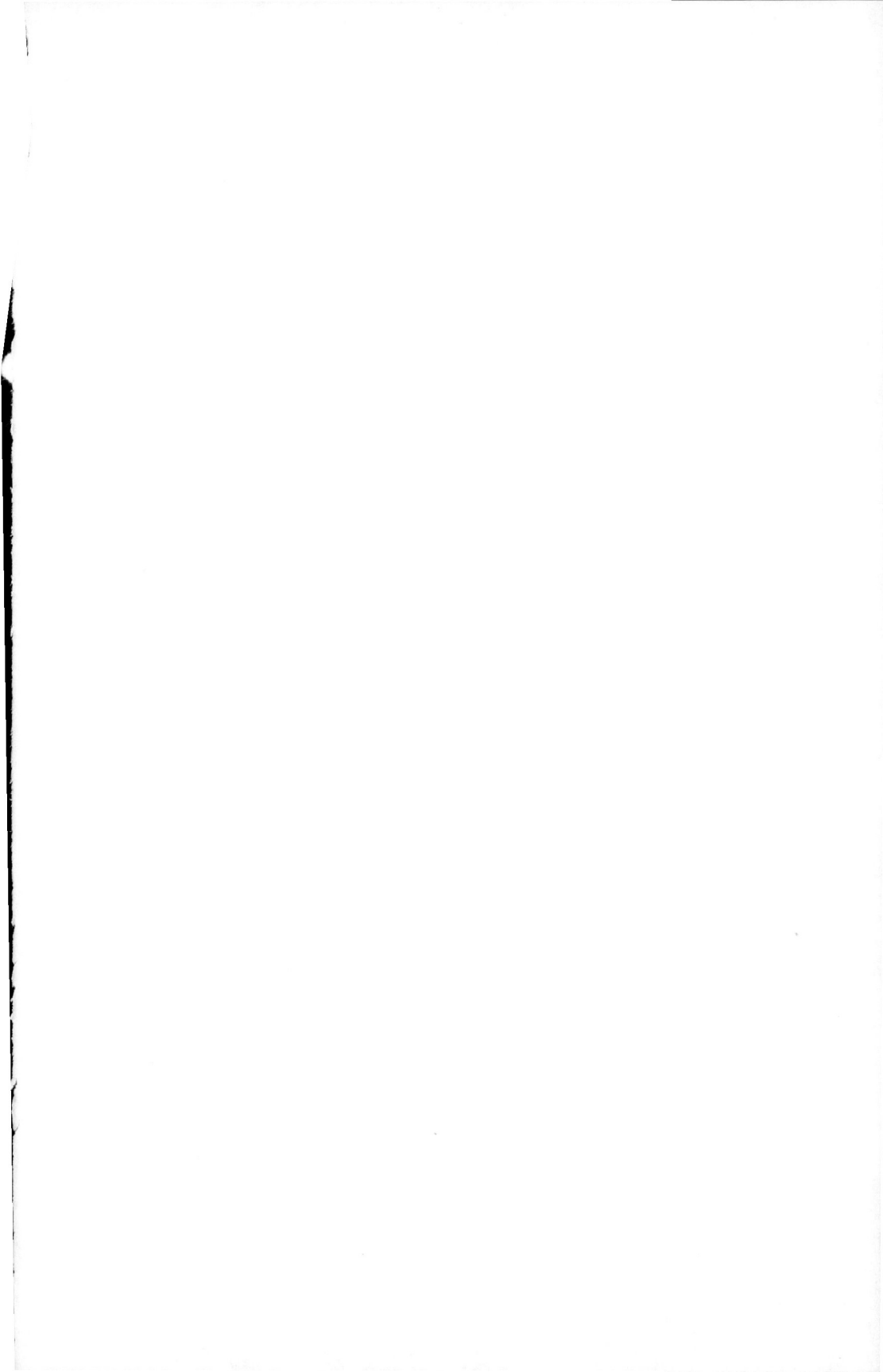